Magnificent One

Magnificent One

Selected new verses from
Divan-i Kebir

Mevlana Jalaluddin Rumi

Translated by
Nevit Oguz Ergin

PUBLISHED FOR THE PAUL BRUNTON PHILOSOPHIC FOUNDATION BY
LARSON PUBLICATIONS

Copyright © 1993 by
The Society for Understanding Mevlana

All rights are reserved. No part of this publication may be reproduced, stored in a retrieval system, or transmitted, in any form or by any means, electronic, chemical, mechanical, optical, photocopying, recording, or otherwise without prior permission in writing from the publisher.

International Standard Book Number: 0-943914-63-9
Library of Congress Catalog Card Number: 93-78441

Published for the Paul Brunton Philosophic Foundation
by Larson Publications
4936 Route 414
Burdett, NY 14818 USA

99 98 97 96 95 95 93

10 9 8 7 6 5 4 3 2 1

Cover image: Khamsa of Nizami. Illuminated circle. Mughal, 1595. Reproduced by permission of the British Library Board.

About the translator: Dr. Nevit Oguz Ergin was born in Turkey in 1928. He migrated first to Canada, then to the United States to pursue postgraduate medical work. He has traveled extensively, especially in Central Asia and in the Near and Far East. He currently resides and practices medicine in southern California, and works with The Society for Understanding Mevlana—a nonprofit organization dedicated to study, translation, and understanding of Rumi and his works.

Introduction

IN THE SUMMER OF 1956, Mr. H. Sushud introduced me to the world of those who understand the purpose of what Sufis describe as the mystical annihilation of self. I had a university degree, was interested in literature, philosophy, metaphysics, and even yoga; but I thought the only way to learn anything was through books. I was like a blind man trying to understand the spectrum of color.

Prior to this meeting, I had practiced some fasting and some breathing exercises—partly out of curiosity, and partly out of desperation in my search for something greater than myself. I tried to summarize for Mr. Sushud the events which led me to these practices by saying, "All the lectures I've heard, all the books I've read, all the schools I've been to haven't changed me. It doesn't matter to me now if I exist because I think or think because I exist: I'm tired of all this mental buffoonery."

He replied, "Some individuals who are not satisfied by nominal, fragmentary truth and not content with science and religion are directed toward *itlak* (the way of liberation) either knowingly or unknowingly. This is possible only through Annihilation." He added, "The sad part is that unless one reaches this Absolute Reality, he cannot understand the nominal or fragmentary reality."

Later Mr. Sushud gave me a few typewritten pages in which he described the stages of Annihilation. To achieve that "decomposing of Being into non-Being," he promised that I would experience lots of hunger, breathlessness, and mental suffering. "Reading, discussing, and fellowship all come later," he said. "First you must do Remembrance (*Dhikr*), Austerity (*Riyadat*), and Contrition (*Inkisar*). If you choose one book," he added, "*Divan-i Kebir* of Mevlana Cellaleddin Rumi will do it."

I soon discovered Rumi's monumental work—thousands of verses in the library of the University of Istanbul, and at the Mevlana Museum in Konya. I was overwhelmed. Reading the *Divan* is like walking in a mine field: it blows your head, your heart, or your soul.

That year, Golpinarli had just published *Gul Deste* (Bouquet of Roses), the Turkish translation of selected ghazals from the *Divan*, with poems arranged by subject matter. This was easier for me to read than the thirteenth-century colloquial Farsi works, and more easily available to buy.

When I saw Mr. Sushud a few weeks later, *Gul Deste* was under my arm. I confessed to him that even though I sensed something here, I did not understand the book. It was late afternoon, and through the half-open curtain in his room I could see the rose bushes in his small garden. He went out, came back with a single long-stemmed rose, and gave it to me. I pressed the rose inside my copy of *Gul Deste* in memory of him.

The book (and the rose) traveled with me to different cities, countries, and continents. I read and tried to understand it, time and again, for three decades without success. During these years, at least half the time I practiced regular fasting and suffered intensely through losses, failures, and humiliations. In the mid-80s I began to smell the real rose in the pages of the *Divan:*

> O, the one who wants
> To smell my fragrance,
> You must die first.

> Don't look for me
> When you are alive.
> I am not as I appear to you.
>
> (HM, g46, v485)

I then went back to the *Divan* in its entirety. In the intervening years, Golpinarli had published a complete Turkish translation of all twenty-one meters (44,000+ verses). I began comparing his work with the handwritten Farsi edition of Osmon Oglu Mevlevi Hosan registered as No. 68 and 69 in the Mevlana Museum in Konya, Turkey. The authenticity of some of the verses in these editions has been questioned and attributed by some scholars to writers other than Mevlana. For myself, I have come to see that the only way one can be sure is to scrutinize the verses carefully for the content of annihilation and spiritual abstraction that characterizes Mevlana and no one else. The work of translating his verses as I understand him from both these sources has become the most rewarding and beautiful task of my life. It brings a joy beyond reckoning.

Anyone trying to understand Rumi through scholarly research alone will not succeed. Mevlana himself was a scholar until October 23, 1244, when he met God's Shems of Tebriz. (Mevlana himself often describes Shems this way in the *Divan.*) From that day onward, he became God's lover. This meeting came to be known among Rumi's followers as "*Marc-al Bahraynn*" (from Koran LV, V-9), which translates as the "merging of the oceans."

According to Rumi's biographers Sipehsalar and Eflaki, Shems and Mevlana stayed together for six months in solitude in a small room in the house of Salahaddin Zer Kub. This period is the most important and least understood part of Mevlana's life.

"What a Sun you were, Oh, Shems of Tebriz, that one ray of your light became the Master (Mevlana) of the world."

H. Sushud

Passing from manifest to unmanifest, from relative to absolute, could seldom be accomplished in six months—even among saints and prophets. The process must definitely have started much earlier in Rumi's life, and come to fruition during his time alone with Shems in the house of Salahaddin.

> You were a drop of sperm
> Became blood, then grew
> Into such a beauty.
> O human, come close to me
> So that I can make
> You better than that.

BR, g89, v864

When science, politics, institutional religions, philosophy, and cults leave men and women in such a sad condition as today, this invitation is probably the only viable alternative for some—provided they are privileged to be offered, accept, and go through the process of annihilation as Rumi shows us. In his words, "Annihilation is the salve of saints." Whoever can obtain it will observe Divine secrets and endless truths. Through "Annihilation of Action," Soul will be discovered. Through "Annihilation of Attributes," Absolute Love will be experienced. At the end is "Annihilation of Essence," which is Annihilation within Annihilation. This is the greatest gift from God to humanity.

Nevit Oguz Ergin
VALENCIA, CALIFORNIA
APRIL 1993

Acknowledgements

MY THANKS TO Paul Cash for selecting and arranging these verses from throughout the several meters of the *Divan* that I have translated so far, to Tim Smith for his valuable suggestions for refining their poetic form in English, and to the great ladies who give me always a helping hand, Ms. Peart and Ms. Alexander.

Also my profound gratitude goes to Professors S.H. Nasr and William C. Chittick for the encouragement they have offered me in this gigantic undertaking. All I pray now is that God will allow me to finish translating the *Divan*, the most rewarding and beautiful task of my life.

1. Come, let's talk to each other
   Through the Soul,
   Saying things secret to the eyes and ears.

   Let's smile like a rose garden
   Without lips and teeth.
   Let's converse through thoughts
   Without tongues or lips.

   Let's tell all the secrets
   Of the world until the end
   Without opening our mouth,
   Like divine intellect.

   Some can only understand
   By listening and by looking at mouths.
   Let's stay out of their tent.

   Nobody talks aloud to themselves.
   Since all of us are one,
   Let's talk that way.

   How can you tell your hand, "Touch"?
   Since all hands are one,
   Let's talk that way.

   Hands and feet know what the Soul wants.
   Let's shut our mouth and talk through our Soul.
   The Soul knows fate, step by step.
   If you want, I'll give examples.

2. Choose Love, Love.
Life without that beautiful Love
Is only a burden,
As you see.

As you see,
The joy and glory of the world
Boasting in the heart of lovers
Is a shame and a disgrace.

Your Love called me aside and asked,
"Why are you passing by and not stopping?"
Then your Love told me, "Look at me carefully.
It is me you are seeing everywhere.

"I am your food, your halting place.
I took your heart.
If you save your Soul from me,
That Soul won't do you any good."

3. O, people, embrace Love.
Respond to its calling.
Run to Him,
Because God gave immortality
Only to Love.

Today, sleepless Love is in the sky
Calling the sleepy Hearts.

Love is the life and feeling
In the universe.
Life without Love
Is only an empty shell.

The one who takes you
Away from Love to earth
Is not your friend.
He is your enemy.

There is no talk in Love.
Moaning and groaning is enough,
And patience is the only thing
Which saves Love.

Be silent. Don't say anything.
Let your tears tell all.
When the Heart starts burning,
It smells like incense.

4. No one has ever reached the Lord
With horse and armor.
We gave up our horse and armor,
Then reached the Lord.

We poured lots of tears
On this soil, like clouds.
We gave up the clouds
To reach that moon.

O drum players, play, play.
Our turn has come. Play, play.
O Turk, come out.
We've reached the place of the tent.

Like Joseph we stayed
At the bottom of the well for some time.
Then, a rope came from that side
And we climbed from the well.

We kept breaking idols
In front of Muhammad,
Until we reached the Beauty
Who is the desire and direction of the Heart.

Come close. We came from a long way.
Ask us how we are doing,
Because we came from the road.

5. There is a sea that is not far from us.
   It is unseen, but it is not hidden.
   It is forbidden to talk about,
   Yet at the same time,
   It is a sin and a sign of ungratefulness
   Not to.

6. I won't tell your secret.
   That would be just telling a tale.
   Instead, I will untie your knot
   Without saying a word.

7. Love has a bunch of keys
   Under its arm.
   Come, open the doors.

8. There is no salvation for the Soul
But to fall in Love.
It has to creep and crawl
Among the Lovers first.

Only Lovers can escape
From these two worlds.
This was written in creation.

Only from the Heart
Can you reach the sky.
The rose of Glory
Can only be raised in the Heart.

Only from the Heart
Can a road be found
To the Beauty who stole your Heart.
Only with the Heart
Can one escape the burden of the body.

The Heart is cooking
A pot of food for you.
Be patient until it is cooked.

Shems of Tebriz is
The Heart of Hearts.
But bats cannot see the sun.

9. The news came, saying,
   "Good fortune brought a Beauty
   Whose face is brighter than the moon
   To the circle of Lovers."

   That Beauty filled
   The Hearts and eyes of Lovers so much
   That names and stories of old Beauties
   Were all forgotten.

   So many fountains of life
   Flew out of that Beauty.
   So many heads and eyes became dizzy
   From that wonderful wine.

   When the moon saw His attack,
   It hid behind the trenches.
   It even had a sword and shield.

   They asked me, "What did you see
   In God's Shems of Tebriz?"
   I told them, "He is a luminous gaze
   Which fell in my Heart."

10. He is the One
    Who rules the Heart and Soul in this town.
    He is the One
    Who rules like the fate of God.
    Hundreds from the glory of faith
    Have fallen and worshipped in front of His face.
    Where is the cloud of doubt
    That will find the way to His moon?
    Like the darkness disappears under
       the moonlight,
    Hundreds of me's and you's
    Will be annihilated
    By the light of that Beauty
    Who has freed Himself from the self.

    There is no temple of peace for the destitute
    But His temple.
    There is no wish or desire
    But the shade of His face
    Which resembles the sun.

Listen to a few words that attempt to
   describe Him:
"I don't have enough power
To say He is such and such."
Yet if I don't tell His name,
If I don't describe Him,
The bottle of Soul will be broken by this wine.
Go ahead.
Your hand shouldn't tremble.
Do take this glass of Love.

Drink.
Since you have the antidote,
Poison won't hurt you.

11. If you are a believer,
    He is searching for you.
    If you are a disbeliever,
    He is calling you.
    Walk this way and become faithful.
    Go there and become unfaithful.
    Both are the same for Him.

12. He has no enemy.
    His drunks are all around.
    Don't stay in the land of solitude.
    The day the parade comes for Lovers,
    Walk in the front. Be a leader.

13. You made an oath
    While you were still a Soul.
    I wonder if you could remember that.
    If you denied that,
    I could wait patiently
    Until the day of Judgement.

14. You were a drop of sperm,
    Became blood, then grew
    Into such a beauty.
    O human, come close to me,
    So I can make you better than that.

15. To decay in the soil
    And be reborn from the soil
    Is for animals,
    Not the Soul.

16. For a time you were fire, then wind,
    Then turned into water, then soil.
    In another time you became animal
    And went through the entire animal kingdom.
    Since you are a Soul now,
    Try to be worthy of the Beloved.

17. Wake up. It is morning time;
    Time to drink the morning wine;
    Time to get drunk.
    Open your arms.
    The beautiful Beloved has come.

    Come and see this magnificent, immortal life.
    This life has been exempted from the
       numbered breath.

    Before, fortune used to scratch our heads.
    It's over.
    From now on, O Heart,
    You scratch the head of fortune.
    The sky which has hundreds of moons
       starts turning.
    O, poor sky, you have nothing but
       one day of shining.

    This glass of Soul
    Which becomes death for the angel of death
    Gives no upset stomach, no dizziness or
       headache.

    Enough. Be silent.
    If Soul depletes our shapes and forms,
    It will bring hundreds of apologies to the
       Beautiful One.

18. This is the kind of wine
    That has a light which reflects the sky
    Which is not supported by poles and walls.
    If you drink a drop of it,
    You will understand all the exuberance
        of my Soul.

    This wine affects your insides,
    Sharpens your mind,
    Enlightens your eyes, your Heart,
    So that in time,
    You will see the pearl
    Inside of this flimsy body.

19. The word comes from Soul,
    But is embarrassed in front of Soul.
    The language is embarrassed
    With "pearl" and "shore"
    Because it is unable to explain them.

    To know and talk about wisdom
    Is an honorable torch.
    But in front of the Sun of Truth,
    They become embarrassed and disappear.

    The world is like foam.
    The sea is like God's attributes.
    Naturally, the foam of the world
    Is embarrassed by the pureness of the sea.

    Clear the foam
    In order to reach the water.
    Don't bother with the foam.
    It is all embarrassed by the sea.

    Don't pay attention
    To the appearances in the earth and the sky,
    Because all the shapes in the earth
    Are embarrassed.
    All forms appear in time
    And are ashamed.

Crack the shell of the letter
In order to understand
The meaning of the word.
Hair is lovely,
But it covers beautiful faces.

Every time you imagine something,
You think you lift the curtain
And find the truth.
Your imagination is really your curtain.

This world of Nothingness
Is the sign and proof of God,
Even though it covers the Beauty of God.

Existence is a favor of Shems of Tebriz,
A favor to the Soul.
But it covers the essence
And is ashamed in front of the Essence

20. You've eaten a few spoonfuls of food
From the pots of this earth.
Don't worry. The rest of it is the same.

My wish is God.
My disciple is God.
I give my old to God.
I give my new to God.

I have been laid down under the feet
Of His fate and accident.
The pavement underfoot doesn't care
About cleanliness or dirt.

There is neither good nor evil
Beside the greatness of God.
Even if one breath separates me from Him
It is not good for me.

I cannot pull myself from His comfort,
Nor from His torture.
God's wish makes me a lock sometimes,
At other times a key.

Even when I blink my eyes,
I cannot take my eyes away from Him.
The things I have now, the things I had before,
They are all His.

He is the mirror's eye.
My Soul, my body become beautiful
With that eye.

21.   O featureless Beauty
      Who creates all features,
      O Cupbearer who offers
      The cup of mischief to Lovers,
      You shut my mouth so the secret can't be told.
      But all those secrets
      Are coming out through the door
      That You opened in my Heart.

      When your beauty secretly dropped the curtain,
      Heart had fallen to the Cupbearer,
      Had agreed with the wine.
      Soul was unable to see
      Your bare face without a veil;
      It doesn't have the power.
      Whatever I say,
      Your beauty is beyond that.

22. The table has been set; the door has been opened.
Quick. Get into the house as a drunk.
Why are you waiting for an invitation?
Even if there is wine, a candle and merriment
All over the world
There is a different touch of Love
In God's drunkenness.

Even if there is plentiful food and drink
Inside of this cage,
Where is the joy and pleasure of the birds
That fly in the sky so freely?

That's also gone.
O the one who will never pass, never go,
Pick up the jar of faithfulness.
You are the Sultan of faithfulness.

Turn the glass of bravery, worthy of the Sultan
So the Soul becomes beautiful,
So Soul plays with Soul and reaches immortality.

This is not wine made by grapes
That makes the stomach upset.
It comes from God's hand.
It's a gift from His jar.

O My Eye, both worlds' eyes are bright
Because of You.
Give me a big cup. Save me from death.

23.   You'll wake up
      From the drunkenness of this world
      After a good's night sleep.
      But the drunkenness from God's wine
      Will last beyond the grave.

24.   Love hasn't seen anyone
      Who is as silly a fool
      As I am in this town.
      He grabbed me from the top
      And pulled me up.
      Any choke, any grab, any pull
      That comes from the top
      Is good.

      Any rebuff from the doorkeeper
      Is just protection.
      He says, "Go away,"
      But that means the Sultan is at home.
      Don't ever go away.

      Don't put anybody before our Beloved.
      There is nobody like Him.
      Don't talk so foolishly.
      He's a clean, pure mirror.
      If you see badness and faults,
      You are the bad one; you have the faults.

You are contained by the earthenware jar.
The more you ferment and froth,
The more you rise to the top.
You have so many wishes
And keep looking for gifts.
Pull yourself together.
You are the real gift.

Day and night you keep having the
   desire of union,
But you are the light of union.
You don't know that.
You don't understand that.

You are looking for a wonderful thing,
But you are the one
Who is to be wondered at.
You are the King and poor at the same time.

25. O young man, the secret is in you.
    Don't ask for it from a stranger,
    From the one who comes and goes.
    There is no use in something
    Which has already been explored.

26. This is such a house
    That music is played and listened to
    All of the time.
    Ask the owner what kind of house this is.

    If this is Kaaba,[1] what are those idols?
    If this is the house of fire worshippers,
    What is this light of God?

    There is such a treasure in this house
    That it cannot be contained
    In the world or in heaven.
    Really, this house and the owner of this house
    Are all pretext.

    Don't look at this house
    Like a house of oppression.
    Don't blame the owner;
    He is drunk from last night.

This house is built by ambergris and musk.
The doors and roof are all rubais and verses.

Anyone who finds the way of this house
Will be the king of the land,
The Solomon of the time.

O Landlord, look down from that roof
Just one time.
There is the sign of good fortune and glory
On Your face.
I swear, anything else
Besides seeing Your face
Is a spell and story.

1. The most sacred shrine of Islam, in the courtyard of the Great Mosque at Mecca, toward which the devout pray. In Islam, it is considered the earthly reflection of the celestial temple which is also reflected in the heart.

27. The Soul is like the mirror
Which embraces Your form.
The Heart is like a comb,
Buried upside down in Your hair.

While watching the Beauty of Joseph,
Women cut their hands with their own knives.[1]

My Soul, come to me.
I'll put my Soul
Right in the middle.

Everybody in that house is drunk.
This or that comes
From the door nobody knows.

Don't sit at the threshold.
It's bad luck.
This Heart becomes darkened
By the one who stays at the threshold.
All of God's drunkenness is one,
Even though they are thousands.
But the ones who get drunk from pleasures
Are only two, three.

Go to the forest of lions.
Don't worry about getting hurt.

---

1. Refers to the story of women who were so captivated by Joseph's beauty as he passed while they were peeling oranges that they cut their fingers with their knives.

28. One has to be alive in Love;
    Death is not good.
    Living one, do you know
    The one who is born from Love?

    The anger of roaring lions
    And the manhood of all men
    Is nothing compared to Love.

    Look for me in Love
    And for Love in me.
    Sometimes I praise Love;
    Sometimes Love praises me.

    When Love opens his mouth
    Like a shell inside of the ocean,
    It swallows the seas of us
    Like a drop of water.

29. The world consumes men in the earth.
But the creator sends us to eat the
whole universe.
The world is a mighty sorceress
Who promises men, "Tomorrow, tomorrow."
Son, we are smarter than that.
We know how we live and enjoy now.

If we were born from a fairy,
Fairies gather at night.
Let's get together at night.
If we are the Sons of Adam,
Let's drink that wine.

We are fish. Our Cupbearer
Is the ocean of Love.
If we drink more or less,
The sea doesn't change.

30. The value of the Beloved
Depends on the level of the Lovers.
O hopeless Lover, what is your value?
What is your worth?
The beauty of the moth is measured
By the light of the candle.
Aren't you the moth for the brightest candle?
O God's Shems[1] of Tebriz,
You are either
The act of seeing or looking
Or the one who looks and sees.
That's why it is impossible
To see and understand You.

1. "Shems" in Persian translates as "Sun."

31. O sea of Truth,
    This earth is Your wave, Your foam.
    You are hidden.
    Sometimes You are busy with work;
    Other times You are tranquil.
    You are neither in the open nor obscure.

    O source of the sun,
    Your exuberance from that sea
    Has pierced the curtain of darkness with light.

    Any dirt You pick up becomes gold.
    Any stone You choose becomes rubies
        and emeralds.

    Whose student are You, then?
    You came into this world as a master.
    Where did You learn
    This trade without tools?

    Be silent.
    Remember how many times
    You have left this world, these thoughts,
    And flown to the door.

32. For God's sake,
    Don't fall in love with another.
    Don't think of anything else
    At the assembly of Soul.

    To choose another lover,
    Get involved with another work,
    Is like an unbelievable curse there.
    Don't join the creed of disbelievers
    At the council of religion.

    Thoughts in the land of Soul
    Are like words and cannot be hidden.
    Don't try to hide them.

    Even if you don't hear the dung beetle,
    You smell it.
    Don't keep any vision in your Heart
    That leaves a bad track.

    The one who guards the Heart
    Gives honors and is very jealous.
    So don't look at strangers.

    Don't make a big deal
    On the topic of your anxieties.
    Don't make all those lost people
    Your guide, your leader.

33. O, the one who has fallen in love with gold
Is yelling and screaming,
As if death won't come
And knock at his door.

Think about the day
You are breathing your last breath
And your wife's mind
Is on another husband.
Before the arrow of death pierces your shield,
Make your aim the commandments.
Surrender yourself.

The purpose of humanity
Is observation and understanding.
O, God's compassion is raining
Observations and understanding.

34. O my God, what irony it is
    That we are at the bottom of hell,
    And yet are afraid
    Of immortality.

35. If the child doesn't go to school
By himself,
He is taken there by force.
O my friend,
Did you think you were an exception?

Pick up the glass.
Free yourself from ties and bindings.
As long as you are aware of yourself,
You depend on questions and answers.

At the end, hear the yells of the drunks.
O you senile imbeciles,
Look what kind of grief you are in.

Let me hold your hand for two, three days.
You'll boil and fry.
Don't turn your face
From the glory of the Kingdom.

Don't fall down and sleep
In the place where you got drunk.
Run to the place of the Cupbearer.

36. You are a chosen, beautiful bird.
    Pick up sweet foods from China.

    You are God's lion.
    God named you men "lion."
    Why do you play with monkeys?

    Don't look at this shape of flesh;
    That's not your peer.
    Of course, now and then even kings
    Wear woolen sweaters.

    Come to your senses.
    Give your heart completely
    To the hand of the Beloved
    So it won't rot with hatred and greed.

    If you're thirsty for fame,
    You get sick with every touch.
    As you can see, as long as you are in this exile
    There is no place and rest for you.

    Mind is like sugar; bodies like sugar cane.
    Meaning is like wine; words like jars.

    Be silent. Don't tell tales of the sea
    To the bird scratching the ground.
    Why do you give a virgin girl to the eunuch?

37. O birds who have flown from your cages,
    Show your faces and tell where you are.

    Your boat has been shattered, wrecked
      on the shore.
    Seize this instant.
    Appear like a fish from the water.

    Either you broke the shell
    And reached Love,
    Or you missed the trap
    And are lost in hunting.

    Today you are either wood for your fire,
    Or the fire has been extinguished
    Because you became the Glory of God.

    This wind either became
    Too cold and froze you,
    Or blows like a morning wind
    In every garden where you arrive.

    You don't open your mouth for an answer,
    But there is an answer
    For every word in your Heart.
    It is salve to the eyes.

38. If you wonder how the senses come and go,
    Pay attention just before the time of sleep.
    That stage unties all the knots
    And shows the truth.
    Organs are like laborers.
    Every one of them does something different.
    The Heart is their commander.
    They follow him.

39. You took me to the door of the house
By telling tales.
You left me there, standing,
And you climbed up to the roof.

You broke a hundred jars of poor neighbors.
You tore hundreds of purses on this way.
Is there anybody left
Whom you haven't put to sleep with your deceit?

You pulled the rug
From under the heads of the people
Who are asleep.
Remember, nobody comes back from that world.
You told me that today.
You've changed your mind again.
You've become like this.

What kind of bird are you?
What is your color?
You'll see today.
You're out of the cage.
Because of the wound
Which death opened in you.

Whom did you let go?
Whom did you choose?
You'll see today. You'll see today.

Either you sucked from the breast of miracles
Or the black devil nursed you.
O falcon, get the turban off
Of your head and face.
Look around carefully and hear well.

Your feet are to take you
To what you desire.
Your eyes are to lead you
Where you can see.
You will smell the roses
That you saw in the rose garden.
The thorn that you put on the Beloved
   will hurt you.
The poison you picked up from the valley
Will bitter your mouth and palate today.
As you can see, your smelted iron
Has become soft today.
You either locked the door
Or put the key in the lock.

At this moment,
If you are pure and clean essence,
You will become a necklace on the
   neck of angels.
But if you are ugly and dirty,
You'll be expelled from the sky.

It doesn't matter
Whether you are the water of life
Or black water.
Once you close your eyes,
You merge with the same source.

If you are freed from self,
You'll fly with the wings of Soul
Among the Souls.
That's what you deserve.

If you reach joy and happiness
With the One who creates joy and happiness,
You'll be away from the black mud of strangers.

The flame of that light
Would buy you back today,
Because you give your Soul and Heart
To buy Him.

40. Since you've reached the sign of Heart,
    Stay here now.
    Since you have seen this moon,
    Stay here now.

    You suffered a lot
    From ignorance,
    Carried your old rags here and there.
    Stay here now.

    Your time is up. You have heard
    All kinds of words
    About the beauty of that Lover.
    Stay here now.

    Vow on your Heart
    There is milk in these breasts.
    You've tasted the milk.
    Stay here now.

41. It is not You who said,
    "I am God."
    It is the breeze of His wine.
    Yet, O Master Mansur,[1]
    Why are you on the gallows?

42. O one who only hears words of Love,
    You should see Love.
    Seeing is different than hearing.

---

1. Famous Sufi executed in Baghdad by fanatic religious partisans and politicians.

43. Today I am in such a shape
    That I can't differentiate
    The load from the donkey.
    I am in such shape today,
    That I don't know which is the thorn
    And which is the rose.

    My Love put me in this shape today.
    I don't know who is the Love
    Or who is the Beloved.

    Yesterday, drunkenness led me
    To the door of my Love.
    But today I can't find
    The door or the house.

    Last year I had two wings,
    Fear and hope.
    Today, I don't know of wings,
    Don't know how to fly,
    Don't know of my lost fears.

44. I wasn't like this before.
   I wasn't out of my mind and senses.
   Once I used to be wise like you,
   Not crazy, insane and broken down
   Like I am now.

   I wasn't the admirer of life
   Which has no trace, no being.
   I used to ask, "Who is this?
   What is that?,"
   And search all the time.

   Since you have wisdom,
   Sit and think
   That probably I was like this before.
   I haven't changed much.

   I used to try to make
   Myself better than everybody.
   I hadn't been hunted
   With the ever-growing Love before.
   I tried to rise above the sky
   With my ambition
   Yet I didn't know
   I was just wandering in the desert.
   At the end, I have raised
   A treasure from the ground.

45. That beautiful Love of His
    Pulled me from my pedantry
    And reading the Koran.
    I fell in Love, became crazy, insane.

    I was dressed with my devoutness,
    Prostrate in the Mosque.
    Piling blessing upon blessing,
    Saying prayer after prayer.

    Then Love entered the Mosque.
    "Oh, reverend," he said,
    "Cut the ties of your being.
    Why are you tied to a place of worship?

    "If you want Annihilation rather than knowledge,
    If you want to go this way,
    Don't be afraid of the wound from my sword.
    Calm your Heart. Put your neck on the ground.

    "If you are free, unrestrained,
    Do these things.
    If you are really beautiful and charming,
    Why are you hiding behind the curtain?
    The beautiful ones have no choice
    But to appear and show their faces.
    They cannot help being adorned and charming."

46. O ignorant one, see your own beauty.
    Know His light of Soul
    At the time of truth.
    Believers are the mirror of each other.

    The soil sees all the secrets
    At the face of the garden
    And wonders, "What beautiful things
    I have hidden in my Heart."

    The stone rises and sees the secrets
    Of the rubies and emeralds
    And wonders what he had in his Heart.

    Black iron finds its Heart in the mirror
    And knows it can shine
    If it goes through purification.

    The ones who become nothing
    Realize the ones who replace them
    Come from nothing.
    They want to get the deed of existence.

    The fly wouldn't land on leftovers
    If it knew it could be a Phoenix
    By working hard.

If a Sufi becomes the son of his Time,
He won't be tomorrow's lazy one.
Fools and lazy ones
Leave their work until tomorrow.

If you are a man and not fickle,
Stay among the Beautiful ones.
Learn to consort with Lovers.

O fish, why are you turning
Your back to the sea
And sitting there?
Try to understand,
You are surrounded by the sea.

Hear the words, "Come back."
Reach the fountain of Life.
Plunge in the water, walk nicely.
Why are you stuck in the mud?

47. Hundreds of new ears
    Opened in my head for hearing.
    Without Someone giving,
    No one could be born;
    Nobody would exist.
    I became a garden and a field,
    A spring breeze blowing to praise You.
    Every particle of mine
    Became pregnant from that praise.

    O, my Beautiful, it is essential
    To clean the mirror of the Heart
    Of superstitions and tales
    With the Love of Your face.
    It is wonderful for drunks
    To pick on each other
    And try to grab the glass of loyalty.

48. I vow
    And vow to the One
    Who abides by One's promise:
    My existence and Absence are filled by Love;
    So are my luck and abundance.

    Wherever there is one
    Who has become dried and like a skeleton,
    Pull him to the sea to rejuvenate.
    Plunge into the sea of exaltation.

    To fall into trouble and to be aware of one's self
    Is the punishment of the stingy, mean people.
    To drink coffee, to get drunk
    Is for the auspicious, happy ones.

49. Don't get in the worlds of subtle points.
    Don't tell stories today.
    Spelling doesn't affect the Heart.
    We don't know stories.

    Our Heart has been plunged
    Into that hair so much
    That we can't separate comb from hair.

    Offer wine. Don't ask too often,
    "How many glasses is that?"
    We remember You
    So that we can't differentiate wine from cup.

50. With Love, we gave up three days, forty days.
Once we arrived at the temple of remembrance,
We were saved from memories.

Be silent! With this Love
And the knowledge Love brings
From God's level,
We are saved from seminaries,
From books and their repetitions.

Be silent! Because of this mine,
This divine treasure,
We are saved from gains, purse and profit.

Come to your senses.
Finish your talk:
Once the sun rises, we are saved
From the watchman, from the thief
And from the dark evening.

51. The devout accepts Your pleasure.
    The wise drinks Your wine.
    Knowledgeable ones praise You.
    Your essence is mine, mine.

52. O Love, You cannot fit in the sky
With Your height.
How come you can fit secretly in my Heart?

You jumped into the house of the Heart
And locked the door behind.
I am the glass of this old oil lamp,
Or the light inside of the light.

My body looks like a pregnant black woman,
My Heart is the white-haired boy inside her.
Half of me is from camphor,
The other from musk.

You are the one who took my Heart.
I pretend to search for it from others.
I reach for things I don't see,
But I am not blind.

King Solomon listened
To the complaint of a small ant.
You also are Solomon.
I suppose I am the small ant.

53. You asked, "Why are you crying?
    You have hundreds of hives of honey."
    I cry at the same time I make the honey comb.
    I wear the same shirt as the bee.
    I won't give a bit of my suffering to anyone.

    I cry like a harp
    Because I am the nightingale of the sky.
    I curl like a snake; I guard the treasure.

    You accuse me of being contemptuous,
    Repeating "I" all the time.
    My friend, I have been away from Self.
    The Self you see in me is your reflection.

    I am raw, at the same time, cooked, burned;
    Laughing and crying at the same time.
    It makes all the world wonder,
    And I wonder myself.
    I am separated at the stage of Union.

54. Once more, the One who answers all prayers
Yelled, "Wake up."
The One who opens the door came.

Prophethood once more passed
Through toward Mecca.
Muhammad came to the altar.
His voice reached your ear.

Once Muhammad came
To the door of the mortal world.
The hole was opened at the door.
The One who opens the door suddenly came.

The sky opened wide
Because of fear of the angel.
Reason came because of the fear of the One
Who creates reason.

55. This time I really
    Got involved with Love
    And separated completely
    From fanatic religions.

56. I don't want mind or reason.
    His knowledge is enough for me.
    The glory of His face
    In the middle of the night
    Is daylight to me.

57. I am tired of the crying
    Of these complaining people.
    I want to hear the roars and yells
    Of the drunk.

    I sing better than nightingales,
    But my mouth is sealed
    Because of everybody's envy.
    Yet I want to scream.

    The master was running around town
    With a candle, saying,
    "I am tired of camels and giants.
    I want to see a man."

    They answered, "We looked,
    But couldn't find him."
    He said, "The One you couldn't find
    Is the One I want."

58. I am drunk today.
I saw a dream last night.
I jumped out of the garden of reason
Like crazy today.

I wonder if I saw a dream
While I was awake.
Because of this grief
I cannot sleep at all.

If so, is this real Love
I saw in the dream
Which I kept worshipping?

Come, oh Love. You are the Soul to my body.
Because of your glory,
I escaped
From the dungeon of the body.

You told me to tear the curtain.
I did.
You told me to break the glass.
I did.
"Leave all your friends," You told me.
I threw everybody from my Heart and
Put my Heart in Your hand.

You wounded my heart.
I was harvesting your shadow
With my eyelashes.
That was my guilt.

Take my life, so I can clap my hands saying,
"I was already tired of this life."

There is a different world
In every strand of Your hair.
Spread them.
I am sick of this world.

Even if I were seven layers deep
In this earth
I would still be in the heights
If I were with You.
Without You, even seven levels of sky
Is hell for me.

59. The hardest part is that You don't have
    a front and side.
   Yet, I look for You here and there.
   You don't fit in any quarter,
   Yet I try to chase You
   From one quarter to another.

60. I took measures. They didn't help.
   The Heart broke its chains
   And dragged Soul
   In front of Your Imperial tent.

61. Since Your shape
    Took place in my Heart,
    Wherever I stay,
    That place turns into heaven.

    All the phantoms, like spirits, have changed.
    Each one of them has become
        a beautiful Chinese woman.
    That terrible neighbor, self,
    From whom everyone suffers so much,
    Has become a very nice friend
    And delightful neighbor.

    The heights have become gardens and meadows.
    Valleys have become treasuries.
    O Beautiful, who are You?
    The whole universe has become like this
    Because of You.

    I was a darkness of the Heart.
    Now I've become the window of the Heart.
    Religion used to stand in my way.
    Now I've become a man
    Who is followed in a religious way.

    The jail of Joseph was the well of calamity.
    Now there is a strong rope for him to climb.

62. When You hide, I am a sinner.
    Once You appear, I am faithful.
    What else do I have after what You gave me?
    Why are You searching in my hand
        and pocket?

63. Since You appear in this form,
    We know this form.
    If You appear differently,
    We will become that form.

64. O knowledge, go away.
    O ear, hear the good news.
    O mind, get drunk.
    O eyes, watch the Kingdom.

65. I have closed my lips.
    Now I am talking with my eyes.
    The drunkenness which won't last
    Is nothing but a burden to the head.

66. Among two thousand of me,
    I wonder which one I am.
    Never mind what I say to you.
    Watch all these struggles.
    Listen to the noises.

    I am out of control now.
    Don't put a glass in front of me.
    When I step, I'll break everything in my way.

    With every breath my Heart takes color
    From your image.
    I am cheerful when you are gay;
    I yell and play.

    But I am somber when you are somber.
    I will be in mourning
    If you put a bad taste in my mouth.

    I will become all kindness
    If you favor me.
    Oh my Beloved, I am exalted with you.
    My lips are like sugar; my mouth is sweet.

    You are the one who exists.
    I am a mirror in your hand.
    Whatever you show appears on me.
    I go through your tests, your whims.
    I become your mirror.

67. If the face of the people
    Were not the mirror of Your face,
    I would run from them to the mountain.

68. Accept this world as Mount Sinai.
    Every moment we want manifestation.
    Every moment God manifests
    And the mountain shatters.

69. I am the One who wrote all this
    On your imagination.
    How can I not know the secret of your Heart?
    I am inside of your Soul.

70. The Soul comes to Love
    As a drunk with his belongings
    Loaded on the oxen.
    "Pawn this load
    At the door of the Tavern," he says.

    The One who gives his Heart
    To God's Shems of Tebriz
    Becomes a doubter of self
    And a believer in the Tavern.

71. O player of Lovers, keep playing.
    Fire the believer and the unbeliever.
    Silence doesn't go with Love.
    Raise the curtain.
    The little baby in the cradle
    Doesn't get milk until he cries.

    My wounds should be an example
    To the people.
    Player, tell them not
    To get in this business.

    Player, name the Beloved
    Who has stolen the peace and patience
    From my heart.

    What can I say? What can I do?
    What has happened to the heart?
    Even if my heart was a mountain,
    It is gone; it was stolen.

    Don't mention my name.
    Talk about Him.
    You'll be the best player in town.

72. O, the one who involves himself
    With this and that
    Without going beyond Self!
    Without putting yourself out of the way,
    What do you expect to accomplish?

    Quit making a web like a spider
    From the saliva of your thoughts.
    That is so flimsy, so fragile.

    Give back whatever thought gave you.
    Watch the King.
    Look for His favor, which was given to you
    Without thought.

    If you don't talk, your speech will be His.
    If you don't knit, He will weave you.

73. O my God! Am I looking for You,
    Or are You looking for me?
    What a shame for me
    That I stay as I am.
    As long as I cannot free "myself" from "me"
    I am someone. You are the other.

74. Self is not a friend.
    It has no loyalty.
    It separates you from your Friend.
    Don't make that double-hearted one
    Your confidant.

    He spills the wine
    And sells the vineyard.
    Don't consider that bitter face
    To be the cupbearer or innkeeper.

    We are at the circle
    Of these wonderful drunks,
    And our Cupbearer doesn't abandon us.
    Don't make us sober.

    Don't advise
    Once the Soul takes over the conversation.
    Don't keep yourself
    Behind the curtain of words.

75. Leave the words.
    Look at the mirror of Essence.
    Because all fear and suspicion
    Come from words.

76. O words, be silent.
    Walk secretly like thought.
    So that the one who thinks, reasons,
        and excuses
    Won't come back and start fighting with me.

77. He said, "If I come, you'll go.
You will be annihilated.
I'll render you into Nothingness.
I cannot fit with anyone in the same place.
That is impossible."

78. Particular intellect is unable to leave
    This fragmented mind
    Because the universal intellect
    Won't be a Nanny for fragmented things.

    If you are a man, don't touch
    Your hand to greed and ambition.
    They are a disease, scabs, thorns.

    If you want to have this door open to you,
    Keep walking toward the door.

79. Don't wait. Plunge into the sea of exaltation.
    In order to do that,
    You must pass out of your self.
    Plunge into that sea.
    It will give you life.
    Once you are annihilated.

    Be silent.
    Walk to Absence on the silent road.
    When you are annihilated,
    You become all praise.

80. If Eve knew your tricks,
    She would sterilize herself
    Because of her embarrassment.

    If the baseness in your soul
    Could be sensed by feeling,
    The whole world would become
    The blackest of the black.

    You are such a snake
    That it is a waste to throw a stone.
    No stone could crush your head
    But your own.

81. Give up cheating, O Lover.
    Be ruined, ruined.
    Jump right in the middle of the fire.
    Get inside the Heart. Be a moth.

    Be a stranger to yourself.
    Come, after you give up your house,
    Stay at the same place with Lovers.

    Go, wash your Heart of hatred seven times,
    Like trays, then come.
    Be a glass for the wine of Love.

    In order to deserve the Beloved
    Be pure Soul.
    If you go to the drunks,
    Be drunk, drunk.

82. Why are you depriving yourself
Of this beautiful valley?
The place where you've spread out
Is no good.

Be the doorkeeper.
A soldier to the Sultan of Absence
So that you will be saved from the
    breath of Soul,
Which is nothing but a breeze.

Don't keep your head in one time
And your feet in another.
Escape from that side.
Watch the drunks. See the ruins.
You are headless. You are feetless.

O guide, if you become drunk with wine
    or wealth,
You guide neither yourself nor others.
The one who has been drunk
Before the beginning of the beginning
Has already been annihilated.
In order to be, one has first to not-be.

83. When Mutezili asked me
    If Nothingness is something,
    I told him,
    "When I am out of my self, it is something.
    When I am with me, it is nothing."

    If you want to put your lips
    To the Beloved's lips,
    Be empty of your self.
    Learn this from the flute reed.
    This thought has led me to such a garden
      at dawn
    That it is neither out of nor in this world.

84. Doing deeds is your sin.
    Trouble starts with your good fortune.
    Your candle creates your darkness.
    All the searching you do is your boundary.

85. If you would get rid of something,
    Get rid of your desires.
    All the suffering and pain we go through
    Comes from our desires.

    I look at His beauty, His rose garden.
    The only refuge for us is His Grace.

    When Heart wakes up every morning
    It washes its face
    And runs toward the place
    It can escape from trouble,
    The place where people turn their faces
    When they are having difficulty,
    Submitting themselves and asking help
        from God.

86. My heart had been torn to pieces
    Looking for help.
    When I understood that helplessness is
    The only help, I repented helplessly.

87. Eternal drunks are annihilated
    In absence.
    The essence of existence
    Is Absence.

88. What a beautiful valley
    Is that valley
    Where only Love walks slowly and gracefully.
    There is nothing but God above this valley
    And nothing but Absence underneath.

89. Love, if you want me,
    If you share my pain,
    If you want to go my way,
    Don't complain.
    Don't have regrets
    Because of your misfortune.

    My Beautiful, don't put on that sad face.
    If you are contented,
    Even the sky will be your slave.

    Greed is what changes
    Your relatives to strangers.
    If a man didn't have greed,
    Everybody would be his uncle.

    Oh, my friend, come and be like me.
    Don't look for prosperity or favor.
    If the devil became like that,
    He would be a king with a coat of arms.

This world is nothing.
We are nothing.
Everything is a dream or phantom.
We are struggling in this nightmare.
If the sleeper knew he was sleeping,
He wouldn't suffer from nightmares.

Yet even if he sees a dream
Full of grief,
If he ever wakes up from his sleep,
He will be engulfed in treasures.

Some see themselves in dungeons,
Others in heaven.
But once they wake up,
There is neither dungeon nor heaven.

What a prosperity is poverty.
What a blessing is the secret of annihilation.
If you experience that, all these appearances
Transform into Nothingness.

90. Be patient in the darkness of grief.
    Don't fear.
    God's help comes
    From the world of darkness.

91. The road to the Beloved gets rough
    Where one falls into the grief of Separation.
    God is the only friend for the Soul
    On the way to God.

92. For the people, His name is Love.
    For me, he is nothing but a troublemaker.
    But such sweet trouble
    That one cannot be happy without it.

    If this world is too small for you,
    Fly to Love.
    Fly to the mountain of closeness.
    You are the phoenix.

    Your body should blaze like a sun
    If you want to shine in the universe
    And enlighten the world.

93. The beginning of the universe
    Is confusion and tumult.
    The end is shaking and quaking.
    Love and gratitude
    Are the same as complaints.
    Peace and comfort come together
    With jolts and shakes.

94. Learn chemistry from the Prophet.
    Be content with whatever God gives you.
    At the moment you accept your troubles,
    The door of Heaven will be open for you.

    Grief is your old, familiar friend.
    When he comes to you,
    Hug him, kiss him, welcome him.
    When torment comes to you from the Beloved,
    Be merry with it.
    That Beauty undresses
    And gives all sweetness after Grief.

    Hang on, clutch the dress of sorrow,
    Because the Beauty inside of that dress
    Is worth all the trouble.

    Grief only sees me when I am smiling.
    I call this the panacea, not the trouble.
    Nothing is more auspicious than Grief.
    There's no limit for its compensations.

God is that Ocean of Grace
Which overflows with gifts
From the worship of begging.
This exaltation comes from
Fasting, praying, and fighting with Self.

Tears do the same as the blood of Martyrs.
The One God who gives the ability to weep
Also gives the way to open hearts.

One thing even better than crying
Is to serve the Heart.
One bit of satin is better
Than fifty woolen things.

95. The grief we welcome
     Turns into joy.
     O grief, come into our arms.
     We are the elixir of sorrows.

     When the silkworm eats leaves,
     It makes a cocoon.
     We are the Love cocoon.
     We don't have
     The leaves and branches of this earth.

     We are when we become Nothing.
     When we lose our legs,
     We become runners.

     I close my mouth.
     I will tell the rest of the poem
     Close-mouthed.

96. Man makes all his plans,
    Takes all the measures,
    But doesn't know his fate.
    Once God's will comes,
    All these plans and measures disappear.

    Man thinks, but his sight is limited.
    He uses all his cunning, but is not Godly.

    If he is successful for just two steps,
    He takes two more,
    Not knowing in what direction
    God will pull him.

    Don't be ostentatious.
    Desire the providence of Love,
    The kingdom of Love.
    That King is the One
    Who saves you from the angel of death.

    Be silent.
    Choose a place to settle down.
    Wherever you choose,
    The King will set you up there.

    You can be sure that all these people
    Are in the prison of death.
    The prisoner cannot get you out of jail.

97. If you're afraid of this fire,
    You will stay raw and uncooked.
    You will be trapped
    If you try to escape from this circle.

    If you try to stay at the front of the line,
    You will always stay dizzy.
    Don't run away from a Friend
    Like you run from the rain.

    Loyalty is the price
    For the assembly of the Elest.[1]

---

[1]. The spiritually mature, as addressed in Koran VII, 172 and 173.

98. If you take a spark from Him,
    Your tongue, your throat will be burned
    And you will start screaming.
    God gives everyone a different morsel.
    Don't look for one you can't swallow.

    Where is the wind of the Soul?
    I will give my life, my heart for it.
    I am not a coward
    Who will give you up for a few troubles.

99. If you are good in Love,
    Don't stay away from ill-reputed friends.

    You are a bird which needs grain.
    All the grain in the world is bait.

    It doesn't affect your honor
    If you hang around with swindlers.
    They are the ones who always choose Lovers.

    In this Love, there are lots of whims.
    Don't show coyness.
    Instead, relax and tolerate.

    O, friend, endure the fire,
    Because after many days,
    Fire will become water.
    Show me the way to the tavern.
    I sold the whole world for one glass.

    O, brother, where are the swindlers?
    If their doors are closed,
    I will drop in from their roof.

    I'll die in front of the cupbearer.
    What a wonderful death,
    To lose one's self and profit from it.

100. Don't complain if somebody cheats you.
　　　You've played a hundred games.
　　　It's only fair
　　　If somebody does the same to you.

101. Man takes measures
　　　But doesn't know his fate.
　　　Man proposes.
　　　God disposes.

102. If your Heart doesn't
　　　Understand being skewered,
　　　That cook will cook you in hell.

103. There is hope after the time of desperation.
There is the eye of Heart in blindness.

You won't know your blindness
Without seeing the light.
How do you know white
Without seeing black?

There are hundreds of thousands
Of forms which look alike.
There are hundreds of thousands
Of meanings and reasons which depend
On this unseen King's secret control.
That King moves these forms and meanings
Like the wind moves the leaves
Of the tree of silence.

There is Love where there is scolding.
Every incomplete thing is pulled toward
 completion.
Try to see the unseen events clearly.
Be silent!

104. Once fortune comes to your hand,
Don't talk about the past.
Laugh at the one who talks
About the past and future,
And the one who listens.

105. All of this is easy
If the bird of your Heart
Has broken the cage and flown to the sky.

It doesn't matter if forms are missing
As long as the Soul reaches soundness.
It is alright if the books are torn,
But the feet are saved.

O the one who doesn't know
The taste of Soul,
Your Soul will give thanks hundreds of times
When it is freed from the torture of this body.

106. Applause! Bravos!
What a beautiful state of ecstasy
Has freed you from other states.
Applause! Bravos!
What a beautiful morning of drinking;
What a beautiful morning of wine.

Even the angel of death tells himself,
"Stop. Your arm does not reach there."

We don't know anything, really.
What is knowledge?
This is the pardon of sin.
This is the forgiveness to cleanse all guilt.

107. If I went out of myself
 Like I did last night,
 If I didn't worry about the troublemakers,
 I could tell the rest of it in ecstasy
 Until my Heart became drunk with that wine.
 But now I will stay silent
 Because I am in myself.

108. Half of the words have been said.
     Be silent. Don't say the other half.
     The sultan of the Soul
     Will spread it to the people
     And make it heard by everyone.

109. There is no word, no ear, no mind today.
     The One who is the base for thought,
     The meaning for words,
     Found me.

110. We have been annihilated
　　 Like a shadow on Your face
　　 Which resembles the sun and Your beauty,
　　 And are saved from all troubles,
　　 O Master.

　　 Come to the bazaar as a drunk.
　　 Look around there.
　　 All the important works will become
　　　　in good order,
　　 O Master.

　　 Telling poems is the only thing
　　 Until the day of death.
　　 Everything else is nonsense,
　　 O Master.

　　 I am silent now.
　　 You tell the rest of it.
　　 You tell, O Sultan of signs and words,
　　 O Master.

Sources

HMM = Hezec Museddesi Mahfuz
MM = Musedds Mehbun
HM = Hezec-i Mekful
R = Recez
M = Muzari
HS = Hezec Salim
GD = Golpinarli's *Gul Deste* (Bouquet of Roses)

1. HMM, g124, v2136-42
2. MM, g79, v7466-67; g80, v7469-70
3. HM, g56, v585-94
4. HM, g39, v419-24
5. R, g97, v1205
6. HMM, g131, v2200
7. HM, g59, v626
8. HMM, g161, v2482-92
9. HM, g15, v177-83
10. HM, g83, v919-25
11. R, g121, v1551
12. R, g121, v1559
13. HMM, g67, v1556-57
14. R, g69, v864
15. HM, g54, v556
16. R, g118, v1526
17. HM, g75, v851-58
18. R, g103, v1315-1316
19. GD, page 302
20. HM, g71, v796-802
21. HM, g63, v683-88
22. HM, terci 88, v981-87
23. R, g51, v671
24. HM, terci 88, v1004-08, 1013-16
25. R, g59, v760
26. HM, g7, v69-77
27. HM, g7, v79-83
28. GD, page 11, v11-12, 15-16
29. GD, page 218
30. HM, g74, v848-50
31. HM, g70, v788-94
32. HM, g19, v202-207
33. HM, g29, v301-305
34. HM, g61, v647
35. HM, g65, v702-706
36. GD, page 327
37. HM, g14, v168-72
38. M, g27, v2373-74
39. HM, g72, v816-32
40. HMM, g8, v973-76
41. HM, g85, v939
42. HM, v60, v635

43. HM, g43, v447–50
44. HMM, g127, v2157–64
45. HS, g59, v740–45
46. HS, g59, v752–61
47. HM, g51, v525–28
48. HM, g71, v807–809
49. HM, g41, v438–40
50. HM, g37, v401–405
51. HMM, g96, v1200
52. GD, page 190
53. GD, page 190
54. HM, g24, v260–63
55. R, g72, v899
56. HMM, g121, v1551
57. GD, page 204, v13–16
58. HMM, g120, v2093–2103
59. HMM, g126, v2155–56
60. R, g116, v1500
61. HM, g23, v244–47, 251–52
62. HMM, g132, v2209
63. HM, g36, v386
64. R, g91, v1139
65. HM, g29, v320
66. GD, page 41
67. HMM, g79, v1789
68. R, g6, v117
69. M, g62, v2682
70. HM, g5, v51–52
71. GD, page 207
72. GD, Page 128
73. R, g140, v1799
74. HM, g19, v215–16, 218, 220
75. HM, g31, v231
76. HM, g44, v468
77. HMM, terci 40, v1344
78. HMM, g12, v1014–15
79. HM, g87, v973–74
80. HMM, g37, v1274–76
81. R, g118, v1514–17
82. HM, g84, v929–33
83. HM, terci 62, v669–671
84. HMM, g71, v1713
85. HM, g42, v442–45
86. M, g53, v2620
87. HM, g84, v933
88. R, g120, v1543
89. GD, page 65
90. HMM, g21, v1128
91. HMM, g66, v1655
92. HS, g61, v779, 786–87
93. R, g1, v10
94. HMM, g284, v3864–69, 3873; g291, v3964, 3975, 3977
95. HM, g45, v479–82
96. HM, g25, v268–73; HM, g31, v340
97. HM, g79, v772–80
98. GD, page 165
99. HMM, g128, v2165–72
100. HM, g49, v513
101. HM, g28, v293
102. HM, g31, v337
103. HMM, g41, v1302
104. HMM, g51, v1396
105. HM, g61, v643–646
106. HM, g67, v741–43
107. R, g131, v1696
108. HMM, g66, v1661
109. HM, g6, v68
110. HM, g69, v666–68, 670